Unfortunately, Thanks for Everything

POEMS BY

T. Anders Carson

✦Pelekinesis

Unfortunately, Thanks for Everything by T. Anders Carson

ISBN: 978-1-949790-04-7

eISBN: 978-1-949790-05-4

Cover artwork: Suzanne A. Marsden
Layout and book design by Mark Givens

First Pelekinesis Printing 2019

For information:
Pelekinesis
112 Harvard Ave #65
Claremont, CA 91711 USA

Library of Congress Cataloging-in-Publication Data
Names: Carson, T. Anders, 1971- author.
Title: Unfortunately, thanks for everything : new poems / by T. Anders Carson.
Description: Claremont, CA : Pelekinesis, [2019]
Identifiers: LCCN 2018057062 (print) | LCCN 2019004016 (ebook) | ISBN
    9781949790054 (ebk) | ISBN 9781949790047 | ISBN 9781949790047(pbk) |
    ISBN 9781949790054(eISBN)
Subjects: LCSH: Canadian poetry--21st century.
Classification: LCC PR9199.4.C38 (ebook) | LCC PR9199.4.C38 A6 2019 (print) |
    DDC 811/.6--dc23
LC record available at https://lccn.loc.gov/2018057062

Pelekinesis
www.pelekinesis.com

poems by

T. ANDERS CARSON

ALSO BY T. ANDERS CARSON

CONTENTS

for V, E and D

Some of the poems previously published in: *Art:Mag* (US), *Canada Post Performance Magazine* (CAN), *Clark Street Review* (US), *The Comstock Review* (US), *The Cracked Mirror* (US), *Curbside Review* (US), *The Danforth Review* (CAN), *Dream Catcher* (UK), *Fire* (UK), *freefall* (US), *Infidel* (US), *Misquote Ink* (US), *Now HERE NOWHERE* (US), *Orange Magazine*, (US), *Ottawa Animation Festival* (CAN), *Our Journey* (US), *Poetry Nottingham* (UK), *The Rockford Review* (US), *Talvipaivanseisaus* (FIN) and *The Taylor Trust* (US).

EARLY MORNING KASTRUP

My young son is safely
out the door.
He has on a helmet
for the bicycle.
He knows the way.
He pedals with such assurance.
One step providing speed
followed by another.
He's got a bicycle
that someone
loaned him.
It's blue.
This morning he was whistling.
The Danish adventure;
in the classroom
on the field
and knowing that
I'm behind him
and a little village back home
encourages him
every step of the way.

PLAYING THAT SWEATING GAME

I awoke in a paralyzed daze.
The sweat was real,
moisture down all sides of my body.
You spend time in the dream zone
and desperately realize that
it is an unhinged mass
that is opened with every key.
Once the eyes close,
slot is opened
and it can begin.
Not having work is not the greatest
for this survivor.
I must clear my moving thoughts
placing one pile upon another.
Finding that eternal peace
that we all chase.
They say it comes
in the early morning
when clouds are low
and the wind is brisk.
I just know that I must
hold onto that gavel
plead,
beg and grovel
that this adventure
is
not guilty.

It has been over a week
and still no job.
It has been a real challenge.
Lots of hoops to jump through,
I've tried to be prepared.
Will go today and take Danish lessons
and that might help my chances.
My son seems to be settling in.
I know what it's like
to be on the outside
as if you don't belong.
We're working through it
as we look out the window
and that rain
very quietly
becomes a sea of hail.

ELBOW PAIN

A couple of months ago,
while chopping wood
there was a pull in my elbow.
It's been hurting ever since.
It wakes me up at night.
I walk with it hanging down
as it truly hurts.
I've tried tensor bandages
and then ice
and that seems to help
and then it reappears
as an old frosted ghost
licking its lemony lips
take that
and I don't quite know
how to shake it
to be free.

IT'S BEEN A COUPLE OF WEEKS

My young lad is on the field
passing balls,
running through drills.
He sits in class
learning the seasons,
makes new friends.
Dad is in the basement lair
waking frightfully early.
Hear the heartbeat in my ears.
Worry of not finding employment.
There is a stack of crisp bills
brought from home
and they are disappearing
almost as quickly as the Grinch
takes small specks of food.

Every day
there are traffic patterns
on the radio.
They must be going somewhere;
doing something.
I find my shaky pen
let it cradle in my firm hand
and write from that
flailing abyss.

READING TO A SON

Every night we read together
sometimes it is funny
other times sad
but last night he said something
as I turned out the light.
A lone street light shone from outside
and he said;
I'm worried about you dad.
That you don't have a job.
That you don't know which team
they are going to put me on.
That you are missing the girls
back home.
I tell him;
We'll make it.
I hug his growing form
kiss his head
and hesitatingly
close the door.

GOING FROM HOME

This is a new life.
without my loving wife.
I miss talking with her
and understanding how much
we respect each other.
She is a strong woman.
There are times when I'm strong too.
You feel as powerful as Thor and
able to solve all with a smile.
But when there is no work
you feel so misdirected
disconnected
and curl onto the couch,
with a book
and try to escape
the brutal darkness
that weaves its way in
through the night.
Pen is the sword
that jousts and keeps
those thoughts
away.
That stringent pen
flowing over the page
as if in unison;
that feared pumping of blood
in vanishing veins.

A MAN WITH A TORCH

I look out the window
and there is a Danish frame;
eyes lulled into happiness
from Tuborg.
His skin warm and shining.
No sunscreen on this
set of feathers.
He is holding a long stick
connected to a propane tank.
He systematically turns
on the gas
it simmers a bit
and then the blue flame.
The weeds singe between
laid stone.
Sweeping back and forth
very thorough
and I can see him
as a boy again
and this time it is night.
The air raid sirens have gone off
and the lights are gone.
Big brightness can cause death
and in an act of vengeance
against a fallen one
he fires up a makeshift nozzle
and storms the guards.

A few will be left
with permanent scars
as his bullet filled body
lies still
quite still,
as still as the plants
that curl away from the flame
that source of heat
a killer
in anyone's hands.

A RUFFLED BOUQUET

It is on the wall
this faded love
that still flows
behind wiped glass.
They were young
but the love was true
all the way
until the end.
This rounded bouquet
pressed in a dream.

IT'S GOOD TO BE BACK

Grabbing a pen and yanking
at the chain
that surrounds me.
It rattles and with this
constant Danish winter rain
it is now rusty.
Sun has not appeared in weeks.
Shoulder and elbow sore
from overtime work
at the post office.
Another bill is paid.
Another slide into the safety
of constant darkness
an urge
a need
a frightened, sweating cry
to hold the pen and let it flow
over the gnawing blank page.

I pull on the white helmet.
I bought it on sale.
You have to do that
to survive in Denmark.
Buy things just about to go off.
Animal parts on the verge of rotting
milk snaking into sourness
and bananas just inches
away from pablum.
But you survive.

Today I saw a rat
scurry across the bicycle path.
I knew it was a rat by its tail.
It was long and the thing
moved quick
so quick.
I told my son about the rat
and he said;
Where?
All major ports have rats.
They are drawn to the moisture
and food.
It's when you see them
abandoning ships
that you know it's time
to learn how to swim.

I slowly pick out those gray hairs
but have no intention
of jumping.
I snap the strap around my bearded chin
and then carefully,
decidedly
pedal out into the frenzied
Danish traffic.

Let's add
another strand
or two.

COULDN'T TELL THE AGE

You know some people
can really point it out,
the age
of cheese
a good wine
vintage film
red threaded Levis
when the Beatles broke up
how many months a baby is in a film
certain muscle cars
the Luke Skywalker action figure
with the retractable light sabre,
what wedding anniversary was missed
but this was different
on a bicycle in Copenhagen
spinning his wheels
sending smiles
opening doors
closing troubled deals
and then when
it's all done
hanging the keys out
touching the door
and saying
I know the age
and it's gonna be
with you.

COPENHAGEN CAN DREAM

Sitting on the couch
watching Rodriguez from Detroit
follow his soul.
In his hands
the trail of anger, resentment
and then clairvoyant epiphanies.
It is right to question.
You must question.
Now on the bed
in the cellar
my suitcase is half opened.
The last trip this black bag
will wander.
Bob Dylan is waking his guru
on the Danish airwaves.
Upstairs my son sleeps
the sleep of the good.
He's following that dream
a ball and a meshed net
which his father rather rolls out.
The words
those sometimes daring words
of persistence
resilience
and never, ever giving up.
That's the road less traveled.
The one with grit behind the ears.

The one that rings just once
on a bicycle path
of this beautiful city.
Get out of the way,
the two wheeled steamer
is coming through
and it takes awhile
but you settle in
and then let
the trembling dream
be free.

A FRIEND ON THE BRINK

The pills didn't help
only made blood pump harder.
Heartbeat scything its way
through the nights.
Curtains are continuously drawn.
Keeps the sunny day
away.
Only the television heals
with its murmuring
and the Danish text
floating across the screen
as if a calming river.
You sit and think
and worry
and that fear spreads.
Wisely you choose
not to accept those pills
into your domain.
A cloud shifts
and you can breathe freely
again.

SOOTHER TREE

Down a back side street
on the island of Amager
is a soother tree.
It is vibrant with colors,
that are added all the time.

I came upon it today
and my first impression
was that it was started
as a reminder of a dead child.
That gave me goose bumps;
lots of them.

Then I thought
what would Danes do with
a soother tree?
I know,
this is where they go
to leave the soothers
as a kind of offering
before entering
into the next stage
of youth.
You leave behind the need
to have ready comfort
and begin to grow that layer of skin
that thickens with age.

Comfort
can only be found
within.

AIRCRAFT LANDING

Two horses gallop
across a field.
They are returning to the group.
They've been running wildly
up and down.
Not noticing airplanes
landing.
They run and run
yet are penned in.
Little electrical cord;
the mom's pushing
their foals to see
if it is on.
It usually is
and that's when they make
a noise.
One that haunts the scarred
night.
That scream
as high pitched as
Lady Castafiore in Tintin.
It could
and has
pierced a room.

You see the airplanes land
into the wind.
You're told
it's safer that way.

AT THE SKATE PARK

There are children kicking
their legs
getting free from home.
They are finding their role in life.
They kick, kick, kick
as frenzied as turtles on their back.
Some with chipped helmets
others riding with the wind in their hair.
They roll up and down the jumps
flying almost spastically wild
into the jungle of mayhem
called adolescence.

SCOOTER

Some stay for the jumps
others wait
for the fall.

BIKING TO WORK

I got to share the trip
with my son.
He's pushing assuredly on his scooter
and I in second gear and
doing fine.
A little bit of a warm-up.

I was at a friend's the other day dad
and I saw something strange.
My friend's dad was out of town.
His mom and the dad's best friend
were over and they were drinking
lots of wine.

It's good to notice things son.
File it for later.

I've done that lots in my life
file it
and we can use it
in an upcoming episode.
Clarity of biking with your son
to work.

AUTISTIC MAN ON BRYDES ALLÉ

Every day for the last 3 months
he waits for me.
I've got a pocket full of doggie treats
but not for humans.
He craves contact
and I,
a little like Santa
in my red coat
give him pails of hope.
Every day he asks
if there is mail for him.
The only ones I give him
are bills.
But this sends him happily
over the railing.
As if wagging an imaginary tail
he gets so, so excited.
when I sadly give him a bill.

As a child he liked toy trains.
He would watch them
go around and around.
The movement gave him solace.

He sees me as a red caboose
going around on my bicycle
always on the same track
and nearly on Swiss time.

Last week we gave each other
a high five.
It is the power of humans
touching
that makes days
just glimmer.

AIR CANADA JET KASTRUP

The Flyvergrillen
at night
engines revving and revving
your body so warm
air-born
once more
gone.

IF THIS IS WHAT BREAKING UP IS YOU CAN HAVE IT

6 months until I see you again

dancing on the kitchen floor

bed so close yet distant

skin has an abrasion

and it must heal

a scar must form

wait, wait, wait

and that big plane

will land

with you.

DATE WITH DEATH

My father died when I was 14.
I'm now 44.
This is how long
he lived.
He wanted to see Moscow
and we went.
He wanted to travel in a VW camper bus
through Europe in '69
and he went with his wife.
I was conceived in the back of the van.
That's probably why
I'm so nomadic
in spirit.
The wheels turning
putting in distance.
In the last couple of years
I've traded that
for a bike.
Yes, a bicycle
up and down the Copenhagen streets.
Picking up milk, bread, toilet paper.
All the essentials
and then you carry them
to your rented home.
The one sucking up almost 90%
of income.
But the kids love it.

Freedom.
They too can peddle
to matches and courses.

Today it's a Sunday.
The sun is out casting
a glow in the kitchen.
It refracts from the candle
near my hand.
So many years ago
my father died
an extremely painful
and cancerous death.
I watched
and it confirmed my belief
that you must seize
opportunities.
You must, must, must.

Those grains of sand in
that ephemeral hour glass
slip through so quickly.
That those dates of youth
become the talk
of the dead
at reunions.

FRESH COAT OF PAINT

My family owned a paint store.
Made some coin
had enough left over
to buy a summer home.
Some businesses fail.
Ours did.

Today,
I'm in Copenhagen.
A friend needs help painting.
Last week I scrubbed around
the oven.
So many layers of bacon fat
and pork having been discharged
on the walls.
I scrubbed my hands raw
getting that grease off
and it worked.
A little elbow power
making one smooth stroke
at a time.
Covering the grime
with freshly chosen
tub of paint.

Beginnings are special.
He's moving out for the first time.
They wait awhile here

almost like in Japan.

Maybe it's the space factor

or the money

but it's beautiful

when it happens.

It's why tears are shed at weddings.

You just want a chance to start again

to listen to the urge

to reveal the play.

Fresh coat of paint

and up 3 flights of stairs

to a new dream.

VINTERGÆK

These are little flowers
that come out
and remind those suffering
from the blackness of winter;
a petal of color
controls the quantity of sanity
that surrounds
a fragile
Northern mind.

ON A BICYCLE

It has a seat
that is always a little
low.
Your lower cheeks kind of
rest on the electric motor.
But that's OK.
As long as you've got two
loaded batteries
you can bike all day.

With assured hands
you've put rubber bands
around each street
numerically and systematically
ordered.
Delivering is the key
with all of that
mountainous sweat.

You ring doorbells
go up long circular staircases
each with a window seat
at the landings.
After the second floor
they have a little
I need to take a break seat
on each level.
They should have heart starters too

but they've been
placed strategically
around town.
Mostly in bank lobbies
where they are most needed.

You bike and deliver
pedal your way across
the rows of streets and back alleys.
You're entitled because
you've got that little postal horn
and a mission to give
and to receive
it all.
Daily.
Just add a stamp.

HEADS OR TAILS

We're flipping on who
had to bike to Dragør
to deliver the mail.
It's a long haul.
You even have to bicycle
under the runway.

Today,
I lost.
It was my first time in months.
Easyjet took off
then Norwegian
after that it was the labyrinth
finding the routes
postal boxes
those little back alleys.
I did almost two routes today
and a gray drizzle.
Hands were cold
until Hotshots revived them.
I found a small stairwell
to stop and have lunch.
It wasn't heated
but it kept the rain off of me
and the wind stopped.
The nice thing was
no thrusting of heartbeats

as on routes with keys.
I go back to my old group
next week.
It's the end of heads or tails.

Tails
and I've finally
won.

TENTED COUGH

I was out on the route today.
The one beside the prison
and mental ward.
From the bushes
came a cluttered cough.
I looked and realized
that it came from the orange Roskilde tent
not a block away
from a new high rise
to house somebody,
but not him.
It was a guttural cough
of many nights
on a dampened floor.
Frost on beards
no chance to ever shave.
Here was the cough
a phlegmatic regalia,
I'm here
but not really here.

Instead
like so many
in Copenhagen;
I push my legs down on the pedals
wanting,
almost sadly needing
some shameful distance.

AGAIN THE FLUTTERS

Running up the stairs
with my parcel.
One step at a time.
not two like my grandmother.
She did that until way into
her 70's.

That little flutter
when you see and hear
colors flashing and siren
the wild homeless man
screaming at cars.
The vision of having
to see them all at the service
all of those ties knotted
just so
prim clothes and
too much make-up.
And the clever way
of holding mints under
their tongue.

It's the way one of the bosses
pressures the foreigner
wanting him to pick up the tempo.
It is the same look as you see on guards
left alone
with too much power

for too long.
It does do something.

It comes this little flutter
and then it decreases
like the air in a balloon
that you let out just for fun.
A flutter will rise
and then go to that
stationed hill beyond
the craning past
and crusted present
and caring future.

One step at a time.
That's what the special book
grandpa had,
told me.
It just didn't say
how far.

FEBRUARY THAW

The wind is up outside
the window.
A dog lays its chin
on the floor.
Native American flutes fill
the room.
There is no one here.
Even the cat is hiding
yet I'm not alone.

The lined up pills are
on my left
my last drink
sits to my right.

Just finished
a short story of Japanese sadness.
It was about a white pelican.
We don't see them here
only the occasional owl
or rare bald eagle.
I look across the room
and see my grandfather dozing
in his chair.
My children aren't playing
in the yard anymore.
Chased off to less frightened homes
they themselves feigning divorce

and distance.
I see my Danish bicycle.
It was a way to bike the pain
of not seeing my wife.
I delivered the mail satisfactorily.

Waiting for her return
as do birders
await migrating birds.
There is also the fastened hunter
powder dry
looking to the sky
waiting.

I rock gently in the chair
as gently as watching my wife
breast feed.
That's what some men
do primarily
is watch.

I rock back and forth
gather the nimble memories
around the room
and sigh,
so deeply
so longingly
as deep as the dog at my feet
waiting
for the door handle
to jiggle.

WHITE SHEET ON A GURNEY

Today
delivered in the three rounded buildings.
Lights flashing and the stern paramedics
rolled the stretcher towards the door.
You don't know which
one it will be this time.
This project opened in the 60's
there were still some Sørensens,
Jespersens and Jensens left
but most have been wheeled out
on that gurney,
the one with the folded sheet
just waiting.

I couldn't slide in mail
hoping it would help,
but ambulances always
do that to people.
They want to see.
They move their curtains,
make whispering noises to family members.
They want blood.

I came upon the door
that was pre-chosen
and there was the white sheet
and they had a blue case jammed in the door
to keep it open.

I gingerly walked over it
placed my letters
in the correct slots
and as I left the building
I placed my hand on the trolley
and remembered the hospital bed
my father slept in at the end.
It was almost at a 45 degree angle.
It's time to do some biking.

That was a long time ago
Mr. Postman.
Don't bring
that overdue bill
to me.

LYING IN BED

It's been almost a week
of a Danish flu.
The kind of illness that lingers
and pushes its stubby hands
on your temples.
It pushes you down.
A snake charmer's grin
lulling you into a defensive
submission
and then the totality
of not being able to move.
Popping white pill
after pill
a racing heart
too tired to even grasp
a rudimentary masturbating
session
head on the pillow
lights
definitively
out.

RED KEY

After biking all day
coming home,
house more quiet
than a lit unfettered candle.
It shines up and bright
house so dark
so cold
so alone
your smile and love
gone, gone, gone.

MY SON IS 13

When we came to Denmark
he was a boy.
We both lived each day
waiting for sister and partner
to come.
We slept shoddily
had trouble concentrating
and had an unkempt feeling.

Now he is almost 14.
Out with friends at a mall
at an all you can eat buffet;
a novelty here in Denmark.
Not all can afford to eat out.
We clip coupons and send them
with the right amount of crowns
so they can pay.

Today,
we'll bike into town
to see an installation of art.
Peddle to the abyss
for in a matter of months
our North American butts
will be firmly wedged into the seats
of a rolling automobile.

TODAY IT WAS THE TRAIN

Tracks are closed,
another one has taken
his life.
Jumped in front of the
first car.
Must be hell
for the engineer.
Must need special training
to come across that
on the tracks.

We'll never know why
just one last step
and then it ended
as regretful as saying
a curt word at a
grandmother's funeral.
No place for that.
Try to remember the positive.
That's why grandma surrounded herself
with Friendship books
dating back years.

This was the first one
my daughter came upon
on her own.

Now we know
the real reason people
want trains to run
on time.

WALKING THE DOG

Twice a week
my son walks a little Chihuahua.
He wrestles with the tiny jacket.
She scampers around the room.

On Wednesday,
as he let himself in with the key,
the owner was there.
She is a teacher and
one of her students
had committed suicide.
The parents were divorced
and she invited them both
over for dinner,
she went up to her room
and hung herself.
A year to the day
when a young boy had done it.
Teenage suicide.

When I was a teenager
I was busy doing the finding.
Once you've encountered that mess
it loses its appeal.
You don't have to rush
the agony along.
You learn to live with it.
Cracked jaws of fear
your jointed fingers popping

as you make a fist.
Suicide breaks you
and no matter how many pieces you pick up
you find there is always
one that is missing.

You spend a lifetime searching
in churches
in temples
in thick jungles
in smoky bars
in books
and you pound that loss
you really pound that loss
with every poem
that you have the courage
to write.
Suicide is the ultimate downer.
Just saying the word
explains much of a disease
and it reveals absolutely nothing.

There will always be a medic
who must cut someone down
a cleaner who must mop frenzied blood
from the bathroom floor
a carpet that must inevitably
be thrown out
but underneath it all
that skanky stain
remains.

BIKING IN AMAGER

On the Amager Landevej
there is a small kiosk
that sits on the edge
of the runway.
It serves, burgers, fries
cola;
all that a man could want.
There is a playground for the kids
when it's your weekend.
It's been my weekend
for 9 months.
I'm the show
for food
clothing,
cleaning,
reminding about showers.

You can sit at the edge
of the runway and watch those beasts
land and take off.
It depends on the wind.
So much of life depends on the wind.
The way people vote,
what color of clothes you'll wear
or if the immigration board
will let you in.
It depends on the wind.

When you get up in the morning,
you strap on a helmet
get on your used bike
and start pedaling.
If the wind is bad
then it's a lower gear
just like those trucks going up hills
in Scranton.

I love those mornings
when you get all the green lights
and the radar gun has you clocked
at 30 km/h
you zip, zip, zip passed
the sleeping Danes
on your way to deliver
their shrinking mail.

I look into my off white helmet
dirtied from biking in a city
and see strands of grey hair.
They've been there for awhile,
the beard a mirrored image of
grey and dark brown.

The wind is blowing.

A SLEEPING BAG AND SCOOTER

It's been there on the road
for four days.
A scooter to help you get around
when you can't walk far.
I bike by it on my route
and each day
it is still there.
It's not far
from the psychiatric ward.
The one with the silent
basketball courts
and tall fences.

There are vines creeping up
to try and depose the
madness.
So here this vehicle sits
on the sidewalk.
No one has taken it.
Not to keep warm
or to tinker with
for a winter project.

No,
there it sits
out in the open
exposed
truly exposed
and at the back
the bungee cord
is red.

NOT ANOTHER TERRORIST POEM

Two shootings in Copenhagen.
Two deaths
defending free speech
and a confirmation.
Is this what it's all coming too?
People gunning down
gathering bombs
exploding in crowded areas
cameras on every street corner
almost a gun in every hand.
Is this what safety is?

When I was a teenager
The Satanic Verses author
had to go into hiding.
Fatwahs called for his head.
Translators killed in Norway.
What is this terror?

Now twenty years on
a gunning down outside a synagogue
on Krystalgade.
On TV at the memorial
you see flowers
children leaving drawings
candles lit to fight back
the darkness.
In the Scandinavian winter

there's enough darkness
of its own to go around,
you don't need to add
to that joy.
I think dark forces
have misunderstood their tactics
as an ant moving a body
to feed the restless beast.

RENEWING A PASSPORT

In my country
they now give them out
for 10 years.
That's a long time.

Yesterday,
I was at the Canadian Embassy
and I picked up the new one.
Updated safety features
new symbols
different codes
and then a photo
that captures a moment;
no smiling mind you
but there you are.
Hair all unkempt
and if you look closely
you'll see the post office
insignia of Post Denmark.
A little horn.
Issued in Copenhagen.

It was the first time
I really looked at
the expiry date
and wondered if I would still
be here
and then after a fretful full moon

rubbing my jaw raw

from worry

not yet

not yet time

not yet time to go.

No need to remove
the axis of light
that melds the purple with blue.
It is an old Copenhagen museum.
The little insects laid out in a row
almost like those burn victims
at the soccer match in Britain.
Not knowing how many more
would be added to the line.

It's almost like the Canadian version
of 9/11.
Airspace closed over the USA
and we started to them land one by one
in Gander, Newfoundland.
Our politicians chose communities
that didn't have lots of population
because we didn't know what
was on those aircraft.
The air traffic controller
in a panic says;
How are we going to accommodate
and the response;
one at a time.

Now it is the dusty afternoon
in March
and the museum is about to close
and those wings
are silent
so silent.

IN THE KRONBORG HALL

It was such a long corridor
in the end my son
looked tired
just walking across
the room.
There was a Christmas tree.
A live one
and presents
and even a little glass ornament
of a young pony.
I loved it.
Vast yet sad.

The king traveled around
the country;
movie star of his day.
Not staying in one place
for too long.
He had people test his food
for poison.

Moon came over
the crest of the turret.
It filled the room with awe.
Some Japanese took photos;
we did too
but it never seems
to do it justice.

Sometimes it's best
to just hold
your loved one's hand
and watch together
sharing the memory
over and over again.

I THINK OF YOU SVEN

The days we used to pillow fight.
The time I visited you on Christmas Day
at the prison.
Playing badminton in the backyard.
Now I don't know where
you've gone.
I remember asking you;
Is there anyone of your acquaintances
that shouldn't know who I am?
you said;
Only one.

That's too many.

Now thinking about the safe confines
of the 10th Anniversary of Mt. Sac's Writer's
Conference
and I can almost think of you
without weeping.

YOU CAN'T HEAR THE FREEWAY

In this park
but one dog owner
diligent
in picking up after
their pup's business.

Across the street
a school at recess
children squealing with laughter;
games being attempted
friends joining in.
Not angry noises.

This is LA.

A couple of blocks over
and there is anger in that schoolyard
drug dealer cruises the street
looking for another customer.
A mini Monroe Doctrine
because this is mine
all of it.
I get it
but sometimes I don't.

I know the cars on the freeway
are moving souls towards
their reflective destinies.
Clean cars,

so clean you can use
the three second rule
if you drop a crumb.

There are less crumbs being dropped.
Hands along freeway off ramps
asking for help
having served the flag
been kicked out of the circle
no one to call,
only heavens can heal.
Photos taken in an afternoon shoot
getting stuck in a tree
and having courage to laugh
at rudimentary fear
of heights.

Are you just going to sit there
or are you going to help
my hopeful mantra
to get through
until noon.

BEING AWAY FROM YOU

It is California again
the sky is beautiful
the students are inspiring
the poetry comes from the heart
and within days
I will be back home
gathering wood
for the next winter.
Pulling back the covers
of love
in our crisp
summer sheets.

There are cacti by the dozens
surrounding the boulevards.
no honking;
all on their way
to somewhere.
Some buying cheap booze with a Ralph's card
others filling up at gas stations
just out of town.
There's a reserve on the outskirts.
For a fee you can go in and
experience the oasis.
It's tropical
in the middle of the desert.
Two winged red dragonflies
hummingbirds
skittering lizards
and tadpoles trying to make a go.
The cars go 5 miles an hour
up the pavement
rocks jutting out
and the smell of booze
all around.
Liquor world and aisles
at the store full of booze.
It's a cheap way to forget.
It's not all who can unicycle
their way through life.

One drink to the next
a real Don Draper town.
Let's meet at the motel
to have sex and steak.
The sun boils down eroding
 moisture of what once was.
A land where sharing was a necessity
not a litigated option.
Palm Springs;
a little oasis in the middle
of the desert
opening it's safe arms
just for you.

IN A ROOM FULL OF PERFUMED SQUALOR

Sitting and looking out
at the saguaro cacti
outside the Tucson fence,
you can see the families
and their waving prickles.
You can see the truthful
wisdom in their bubbling buds.
You can hear them sharply cry
when the season is just too dry.

I see a row of scattered crosses
by the road.
A silly Saturday night dare;
a few too many at Bandito's
yet the saguaro don't judge
like I do.
They've seen it all.
Planes,
stagecoach,
coyote
lizard
bobcat
a cycle of vulnerability.

In this sphere we stare
trying to structurally secure
the here and now.
A clinking key,

a puff of Parisian perfume
and a flag whose colors
will never run.

LAST NIGHT AT DENNY'S

At the restaurant
they asked me to tell of my time
in Kenya
as an 18 year old.
I started to and then the memory
came home.
I was in a Kikuyu family
and my host mother asked me
what a white person's
penis looked like.
I was 18.
She was 35.

I guess it was my shyness
that was apparent.
I danced around the request
and later asked to move families.
Some of the other students
had been raped.
Another got hooked on heroin.
One from LA lasted two days.

It is almost 30 years later
at a Denny's
in West Covina
that the conversation stopped
when I respectfully
refrained
from showing.

CRY FREEDOM

Watching the movie
in the stalls in Nairobi
with my Kenyan brothers and sisters
and I the only white one.

The police didn't
ask me
to move.

GOING DOWN THE STAIRCASE

It's Chicago O'Hare
dinosaur bones, Chicago Cubs goodies
and popcorn in many varieties.
On the plane
a woman let me know that
I had left my book.
Thoughtful.
It's done, I said.
Firmly and then sadly, sadly.
Most likely the book will be tossed
but maybe it will be picked up
and passed on
like we used to do traveling in India
in the 90's.
There was always a book
and even some good ones.

On the staircase
there's a soccer team.
Young girls all dressed in blue.
Numbers distinguishing their places
on the field;
always wanting number one.

Now a cart moving the infirm,
large and veterans
gets another passenger.

He is an old African American soldier
and has trouble getting on.
Two sets of canes.
No one helps.
He's got his boarding pass
and his cammo outfit slides down
and he moons me.

I think of my son in the play GREASE.
He was the mooner.
He did a good job.
They laughed and were entertained.

Now a couple of months on
idling in the airport
awaiting the next flight.
Cammo man is taken away
to his distant gate.
The girls' soccer team is long gone
on their path to greatness
and I'm now 47
fretting a little
every now and then
about finances
what the end will be like
when we go
and knowing when to see
the growing teenage children.

It's the staircase of time
being filled
with each
upward movement
and awaiting
the strength to climb
that just won't come.

ON THE S TRAIN IN BERLIN

I was noticing shoes;
lots of leather ones
people plodding around with cow skin
on their feet.
It must have been this exhibit on furs
at the National Museum
in Copenhagen.
I wandered through the displays,
touching furs and wondering
if I was OK with it.
Being in the Arctic
I know it is needed to keep warm.
Man-made stuff just doesn't cut
the real cold.
I can have the fur coats
stay on the shelves.

As a young man of 19
I worked on a mink farm.
My job was to shovel the shit
from underneath the minute cages.
The smell was awful
and looking on the row upon row
of little pleading eyes;
it was like a mini work camp
from WWII.
I know where fur comes from
and it's not for me.

I know my grandmother loved
her mink.
Every year she would ask her husband
if he would buy her a mink coat
and he always answered;
that will be the day.
She waited patiently and persistently
until his death in 1979
and then she bought that mink.
It was the status symbol
she had longed for.
She had arrived.

I now look down at my own soles
and they are ripped dirty sneakers
and with those comfortable first steps
I plod into my first ever visit
of Berlin.

A BERLIN MEETING

We used to be
in kindergarten
together.
A time when playing with sand
and water stations
were the world's greatest distraction.
We graduated into small trips
in Grade 4 to Quebec City.
We rode in one of those coach buses
long before seatbelts were an option.
We remember driving down the East Coast
like so many in flight Canadian geese
searching for warmth and nourishment.
Now after our parents death
we meet again
this time
the gray fooling age guessers at fairs
and we recoil humbly
into the possible cloak of time
safely and assuredly
bringing us home.

BACK IN LONDON

A checked woman
sits smoking her cigarette
waiting for the National Express Bus.
Late again
her slacks sliding down
and showing her white
British bottom.
One where the sun has
forgotten to shine.
Sullenly she takes puff
after puff
on that stick
hoping that this one
will help stoke
the extinguished fire
within.

PIGEON IN ALDGATE

Sitting on the tube
the little pigeon hobbled
onto the carriage.
Pecking its way
searching for much needed crumbs.
I saw the British lady's
eyes well up.
I've always known
they've loved their animals.
They'll doggedly
push by beggars
and say *they could work*
and *they look strong enough*
but this little pitiful pigeon
hobbling
going underneath the seats
searching.

I wish I had a box
so I could take it to the vets.
The vets have to do something
you know.
That's the law;
she said.

I left the train
wondering how many breed animals
are given in each day.

How many cauldrons of myrrh,
frankincense and asking for ablution?
An animal isn't so far removed
and this lovely soul
showed this hardened traveler
that it's true.
Peace can happen
if we just give it
a wee chance.

CASWELL HOTEL

Found on the internet
carpets a bit worn
daughter wanted to check
for bed bugs
but I said don't
if found
we won't be moving
can't afford it.
It's been that kind
of almost two year stint.
A barrier of geld
or lack thereof
and you have to find
a way to entertain
with cards or playing the spoons.
A wise Indian at work
asked me why did I come
to Copenhagen.

On this sunny afternoon;
a ticket for a play
in my pocket
a busker playing lovely,
sad music
my daughter drifting to sleep
I
the old one

giving her a little nudge
wanting to move on.
This terminal movement
of wanting
to see more.

HOMELESS OF MALMÖ

Outside the stores
they sit
eyes looking down
a picture of dead loved ones
hands truly begging.
My son asks;
What went wrong?
It's just possible
that there was a time
when it had never
been right.

IN INDIA BACK IN 1992

I was in a hotel room.
My shower
must have been connected
to an electric circuit
because I got a jolt.
I let the staff know.

He came in,
felt the little buzz and said;
Come.

I followed him.
We walked
down the hall.
He knocked on a random door
and he looked at me
as he opened it
he said;
Shower quickly.

SITTING IN THE WHIRLPOOL

Looking up at the sky
ORION and his dog
looking down but not out.
Flashing lights out at sea
bobbing up and down.
In harbor
a casino boat
leaves American safety
for International waters.
There the wheel of roulette spins
chips click and sway
and at another table a young man
has doubled down on two nines
and won.

This doesn't happen often
so you sit in a blissful warm flow
you move back and forth
over your right shoulder
and close your eyes
on a sliver
of compressed pain.

SECRET PATH TO SANITY

On the paved road,
these two travelers met.
One,
girlfriend in tow
and the other
tasting life
with all of its nectar.
An unlikely pair
but both speaking
the same '*I understand you*,'
language.
Hitchhiking through Jordan,
leaving Israel twice
and ending up in the lobby
of the Taba Hilton
in Egypt.

I met them there,
carols singing
Christmas trees and fake presents
beneath the branches.
In the past few days,
these two friends
have taught me to laugh again.
There is great strength
derived from good humor
and giggling in a frenzy.
We climbed Mt. Sinai.

Without
that tough Aussie lass'
powerful character,
I don't think I could
have made it.
Now with photo on peak
and stories germinating,
I revel in fate
bestowing
grand heaps
of sanity.

SOLID ARGENTINEAN

Handsome face.
Lean body.
Shattering eyes
that would make movie-goers
faint in the aisles.
This semi-saint
nursed me back to health
in the far reaches of Nepal.
He renewed my faith
in a caring hand
being given to one in need.
He listened to the fantastic tale
of my morbid fascination
with cemeteries, mental wards
and addicts.
I confided in him.
The mountains holds a
secret friendship that
has passed through
the reeds of change.
With grayer hairs
and longer lines,
we look at each other.
Holding hands
we try to remember
a time
when we were allowed
to just be.

SCENTED VIOLENCE

Urges appear
behind Tunisian dinars.
Resting upon slim blades
of surrendered carpets,
they beg to be chosen.
Carefully
the little girls' hands
become numb,
making intricate weaving
for the rich.
In a sudden
scab of brilliance,
an oasis appears
in the middle
of a North African
downfall.

My body
has become coaxed
to seethe in perpetual heat.
I scratch
furiously at the sofa
digging my claws deep
into the New Material Only
stuffing.
I am hurt roaming
through the Medina.
Dogs viciously bark

the Arab lament
to the night.

I kneel,
in front
of the full moon
in Tunis.
Jesting and jousting,
a petal of crazed jealousy
clings to my psyche
like some radioactive
sexless scarab.
I will continue this quest
for sight and sound.
Each seething crack,
lowers my cranial
blood pressure.

Strokes will not shatter
this senile sound barrier.
It will record
a sudden atrocity
as quickly as a Sicilian thief,
only recurring
in nightmares that swing
from unpainted chandeliers.
It reminds us,
that gelling dates
will rot
under any
cooking sun.

A REAQUAINTANCE

In a Northern town,
where there is a medical clinic
for torture victims,
we met over a cup of coffee.
In our teens,
we both came from
the same tight neighborhood.
She is now waiting
for her husband
who's completing
his compulsory military service.
She has changed with time
and is serene.
This small town
has given her much time to think.
Coffee flows.
Cars pass.
The lake is still.
Wind silent.
Mountains surround the conversation
enveloping shared secrets.

With time,
I must awaken
from this daze of morbidity
and inner silence.
With time,

forgiveness
will make the soul
that much stronger.

ROAMING AMOK UNDER FORM 4 FILLED NIGHTS

The beguiled butchery
I witnessed as a teenager,
serves up many a sardonic card
when I least expect it.
The tears flow freely holding onto
that false hope that those ambulance men
could do some valid resuscitating.
It was not to be.
I hold myself in contempt,
as I linger on the unseen and unfelt emotions
that could have spoken wings.
They'd released some of this
formulating process and it made me
hold onto some kind of skewed reality.
That her bold flesh could extrapolate
such fluid still disturbs me.
The color of that water was yellow.
The bowels seem to release when extreme
tension is relaxed.

After living under the fear of
being a bastard all of her young life,
she goes and does herself in
like some Hollywood bitch.
We are supposed to learn from the
past tense of things.

Not build them high
and watch them tumble like
castles in storybooks.
The pirates;
that my father whispered in my ear,
still hold that clouded despondency today.
The surreal village of some gratuitous past.
I fold my fake opal colored flower
and place it at the foot of my forgiveness.
Living alone in the mind
is untouchable.
Living alone in the community
is unbearable.
However, living alone with a torrid
soul can cause break-downs on all
sides of those fence sitters.
Torch the fuckers.

ROWS OF UNWANTED PREGNANCIES

Earrings cling
to a piercing hope
of one day getting
out of this drudgery.
The misplaced mills of Halifax.
Roundabouts
spinning every driver
into convulsions.
The lottery sign as a sacred
pledge to success.
I wanna be in pictures.
I wanna be a star.
I wanna be lucky
cuz' I wanna go far.
Grandmother's scraping eye
walks casually with her
granddaughter.
Inside the stolen Bull's jacket,
there is a 15 year old womb
that is compassionately stretching,
leaving marks of a hesitant withdrawal.
He said 'eed pull it out.
Now picking through Israeli fruit
in a Morrison's Supermarket,
she thinks of having a quick puff
behind the shed.
Black-eyed children

roam the aisles.
Another sits in a cart
crying secretively.
He holds the car boot blanket to his skull
and asks how can he leave
this twisted system.
They hook you with a fancy car
which needs to be parked
in front of a home,
that needs to be furnished,
that needs upkeep.
Banks grin their vaulted pleasure.
Insurance brokers stroke their brows
as police sit diddling
walking sticks
waiting, urging the crowd
for a back street drubbing.
All of this for Mother's Day.
That little dream of getting up
with breakfast in bed.
The hope of having the laundry done.
That smile that says,
Yes you've been a two-faced shit all year
but I still like a good poke once and awhile.
She is resigned to drinking
out of ash-filled beer cans
inhaling Her Majesty's tobacco,
dreaming of a faith within.
Wandering these Northern thoughts,

I am so far away,
that flowers would die
before I could lay them
on her grave.

STANDING ON THE METRO

Smell of incense
and onions
stickles the air.
Body heat protracted
as luscious Arab hips sway
to the bending curves of the line.
They are on their way,
home from the market,
on this Saturday afternoon.
Some to see their lovers
others to bake bread.
Some to care for
the sick uncle.
You never see them
smoke in public.
They don't have the
jagged prayer calls.
In defiance,
the elderly hold their veils
in their teeth.
It keeps them silent.
I think that when I ask for directions,
meeting their curious gaze,
they feel embarrassed and almost blush.
I keep my mouth shut
as the Arab tongue
caresses every corner
of our tram.

SOUR PILGRIMAGE

I caress the idea
of Jerusalem,
hoping it will become clearer
and it has.
The Holiest of Holy
is not for me.
All of those misspent hours
in the basement of mom's church.
All the supposed forgiveness
for countless sins.
All of the culled ideas
of Holy Land clarity.
It is a city like no other.
Failing to clutch the crux
of humanity,
I can only wish this place well,
for,
yes,
I am too sensitive
to live with guns,
tickling my spine,
on an intercity bus.

THE RAILING

Traffic sucking its red light gloom.

Pigeons shitting at the moon.

Dusty boxes of cement

under a fresh sheet of plastic.

Sunshine at the window.

A child asleep in the room.

A father cries in anguish.

His fear of heights is relinquished

with each step he takes.

A cover must coat the window.

His fear of jumping from the railing and

tumbling headlong

into an under-powered Renault.

A Paris railing,

the only thing between distance

and suffering.

ON AN EAST BOUND PLANE

Covered in sweat
from moving luggage of 30 players;
a bus from Ottawa to Montreal,
four way blinker on the highway
broken.
Not this chaperone
time for a dutiful plan B
another bus appears
parks in front
air conditioner works
it's cooling dream.
Back on the highway
French Canadian Jacques Villeneuve bus driver
gets us there on time.
We unload and check in
no longer human
just machines.
A couple of token humanoids
to guide and help press buttons.
Within minutes another line up
without a soul scanning our tag.
Luggage leaves our hands
and then boom it's gone.
Going through security
another random check
hands, navel, and feet
swabbed so swiftly.

It's the security that keeps it real.
It heightens suspicion.
As we sit down
turkey soup on all the screens.
Whose behind this curtain?
Sitting on the comforting KLM
with a blue blanket
surrounding my scars
it begins;
this adventure
this nebulous trust.

My head pounded last night.
For the first time in months,
I passed out at 8 in the evening.
The 4:30 light
is creeping in behind
the dusty curtains.
I can barely breathe.
Flakes of plaster
chip off the ceiling
and land
in my hair.
I put the pieces
on an old postal scale
and realize
that in 1945
I could have sent it
to India
for 4 pennies.
I can barely get it out of state
for that price today.
Headaches pass
as do burping babies,
neck injuries from car accidents
and herpes.

In the next few weeks,
I'll be visiting Montreal,

the local mental hospital and
a retirement home.
Not necessarily in that order.
I'll also will begin to deal with
the death of my mother
in a more humane fashion.
I wipe the asteroid
out of my eye,
shake out an old pair of jeans
and put on my musty socks
for survival.

CUTTING THE TREE

We heat with wood.
It needs to be gathered
a year in advance,
so it can dry.
We burn everything
poplar
birch
oak
iron wood
maple
red pine
white pine
ash
and fire starting
cedar.

My wife and I wear
the gear wisely.
Don't cut in the rain.
I love the smell of the two-stroke.
It reminds me of my great aunt's
wooden boat.
It was always full of water
but the smell was charming.
She would take us out
for trips into Portland
and sometimes give us candy.

One time at their winter place
in Daytona Beach
she gave both my brother and I
a roll of quarters
for the boardwalk.

I lost respect for her in my teenage years
when I shared the story of a black girlfriend
I had from Jamaica
Get rid of her
and the racism seethed out of her.

I'm glad that didn't stick.
Rain is falling on our tin roof.
The light is on across the way.
I must find his number
to let him know that he forgot
the light.

It's cozy by the lake.
A cat is purring and licking.
A woman is dreaming and
her naked leg is exposed
and the Canadian geese
are calling in the dark
waiting to go.

IT HAS BEEN MONTHS OF SILENCE

A cat purrs
on my single sheet.
Fan spins its July staleness.
She is quiet again tonight.
Her heart has beaten
enough.
Love but a frail veil
over time.
With the cowardice
of a combative priest
hollow words
and moist encounters
narrow vividly
in the seething rain.

TODAY I OPENED A DRAWER

Mouse droppings
in a cottage.
You know
it's been dormant
all winter.
I've always been a little apprehensive
of opening drawers.

There can be old photos
that strike Greek god like fear
or possibly naked photos
of your parents.

Once you've cleaned out the past,
it's the drawer that is closed
that's enticing.

I want to open it
but wait until I'm ready
for that little cradle
of objects
to burn and burn
and burn.

FORGIVE ME

For the inane way I have of trying to comfort.
My father couldn't.
I learned wrong.
That's right.
I learned wrong;
for the way she would control
your every desire;
that was wrong.
She had to let you want it.
Whatever happened;
to share
to working it out
to working on it together.
No future begins with one.
Push yourself away from land
long enough
and you'll parch in the heat.
Even your urine can't help you.
Flames realized your nightmare.
A pyre of a Viking
that burned
my soul.
Forgive me for sometimes
hating you.
Your wake is just
too great.

ANNIVERSARY

Mom decided to surprise dad.
Had an old antique boat pull
up to the dock.
80 guests invited.
Marriage vows renewed.
The thing was
that he didn't know.

I was 12
watching the kids
run through the forest.
Adults filling glasses
food spilling over plates
and my dad looking at me
for guidance.
Her illness
becoming more acute.

I knew then
that it was
only a matter of time.

UNDERWEAR STILL ON

It still comes to me,
at 4:30 am.
Images of my mother
moving back and forth in those bubbles
in the tub.
Flashing lights.
My hurried 911 call.
I was so nervous.
I even hung up
and they called back.
Fire department first to arrive
then later the ambulance
and questioning police
wondering if it was murder.
Her underwear was still on.
I don't know many people who
bathe in their underwear.

It's amazing what a bottle of pills
mixed with booze does
to a family.
It splinters them
like dropped glass
in the kitchen.
You sweep it clean

but there is always one shard
that you miss
and it embeds itself
in the sole of your foot.

TWO COPS IN THE DRIVEWAY

It has been years
since they came into our house.
Removing mom,
protecting her from herself.
Officers in uniform forcing
her head into the back
of that cruiser.
Her venomous stare
and the bodily hunger
to be with family.
Many officers,
many cars
and then that unprecedented
silence in the house.

As if in an airport terminal
after the security check.
No man's land of anywhere.
Just a vacuous place
to glide in the memories
and jockey for sanity.

Now they are at the door again.
This time they had a call
because someone suspected a break-in.
Those badge numbers,
the weapons neatly on hip
one was a lefty

and answering questions.

Scribbling numbers in a pad.

Those painful memories rekindled

with a brisk

yet firm stroke;

over the flame.

FEELING DISTRAUGHT

It's happened again;
a blackout.
It doesn't mean that it needs
to be serious
or even controlled.
This one is not explained
by the specialists.
This one is full of mutated
mystery.
This one must be solved
with a panicked,
frightened hand.
This one must be helped.
This one is valuable.
This one will make considerable
changes.

Let this one be free
of suffering and pain
for she has already
swum in the torrent of
puzzled denial.

She has tread water
when it has risen.
She has swallowed every crumb
when the food made her sick.
This one is in need

of understanding.
Let the lab coats test
for the right thing.
Enough prying and prodding.
The dam needs a controlled
burst.
The dam needs to be reinforced.
The dam is holding it all back.
This one will fly.
This one can see.
This one will understand.
Let her gently be.

SOMETIMES

I knew I had it right
when grandma said;
You need to come now.
I got on that plane.
They say you cross the Atlantic
seven times before they go.

I sat in the room.
It was April
much like a sunny day
in Southern California.
A circus was in town
and there was an accordion
playing.
It would be five days
before you went.

That last image;
an empty bed
an indented pillow
and the candle burning
brightly before noon.

SUNDAY TELEPHONE CALL

I hear her voice on
the phone denying
longing and hope.
In a couple of weeks,
she's going to have
another operation.
It's that damn eye that
won't co-operate.

Last March,
when packing up her house,
I placed her fake X-mas tree
and the wreaths
my father made as a teenager
in a box.
She opened it
a few days ago
and cried.
I asked her if she had
heard from my brother.
She said no,
only another hang-up
in the night.
At times,
she can hear his breathing and
silently whispers his name.
A tone interrupts her attempt

and she becomes restless.
Blood pressure high,
weight down,
outlook glum.

Moving my grandmother
into a home
was a difficult
thing to do.
Without her compassion
I would have never finished
the packing.
It's something we can't deny
in North-America.
Dad will die.
As will Mum.
But the hardest is that
first one.

It could be a goldfish,
a dog named Butch
or a cat called Scraps.
Maybe Aunty Edith
or Aunt Mabel
possibly Uncle Richard
but if it is a grandparent
that loves you without prejudice,
the parting is intense.
Guilt of not visiting as oft
or missing the signs

creeps into our psyches.
Coping with this regret
is of an utmost importance.

I only hope
that my grandchildren,
won't deny my existence
when I leave
this bodily form.

MARSHMALLOW

That was the last time
I saw my grandfather
smile
was when he put,
with his shaking hand,
marshmallows
onto my whittled stick.

O BROTHER

I'm attempting to write about
you again.
The Brother
Karamazov
Dickens
Twain and all the other wonders
of rivalry and its subsequent
destruction.

He rolled his '96 Dodge Ram
6 times this past weekend.
Brushed off the glass and
walked home.

Two days later after having
rented a Chrysler LHS
he smacks into a car
as he was headed to the detox center.
He left the scene of the accident
and an ambulance was called for he
was on the verge of overdosing.
I drove up last Thursday to see
if I could see him but he had been
subsequently discharged.
I found him detoxified and still shaking
and took him to the local donut hole
for a chat.

I asked him if he was coming back
and he shook his head no.

I've done a lot of thinking in the past 6 years
about my mother's suicide.
I don't care what the Federal Law is;
if a person wants to die by their own hand
I believe they have a right to do so.
I will have to try and package the sorrow
of my mother's untimely death at 49
and roll with my brother's oncoming
disaster.

I understand if the pain is a tad
too much to bear.
He opted to use street drugs to dull the pain
and I write sometimes unwillingly.

I take my rotten carrot slicer
and gently grind it down
to where my nails grow
and then throw it
in the flames.

ANOTHER LETTER

He's coming to terms with
being behind bars.
His soul on the page
with every word and spelled
thought.
He is sharpening his skills
of CPR and will
avoid mouth to mouth
but will share a needle.

Far away bombs go off
in a capital I once knew.
Now I'm afraid
I know nothing.
The letter will come
just as the bombs will detonate
again and again and again.

I close my eyes on his harshness
and twisted pleas.
I am a muted soldier
of misfortune;
as I hobble
hand in hand
on the curled cry
of the walking wounded.

IT'S BEEN A MONTH OF COLLECT CALLS

Yes, I accept the charge.
A facility in Edmonton,
your anger so,
so present.
The guards glaring at you
as you switch into broken Swedish.
The calls are recorded
as if for some recording studio
and there's a maestro
waiting for the next big hit.
This time
it's what warrants solitary
less food and taking the books away
even those
with Biblical leanings.
The church ladies don't like
that it's better
when all is forgiven
with furnished wombs
rolled antique carpets
tattered at certain edges
and cigarette holes
in the chair.

He doesn't listen
only opens
his Kerouacian conscience

and tells all about
how the animals speak to him
and they hear.

Sometimes,
I wonder if my heart
can answer
those collect calls.
A wave of nausea
followed by the brazen realization
of what must be.
Yes, I accept the charge.

IT HAS BEEN YEARS

I haven't heard your voice
brother.
Last time,
only a threat.
I still remember meeting you
then on the street
in Edmonton
not totally gone
gathering two sandwiches from
the shelter,
one destined for me.
It's hard to see the sun going
down on that sadness
we deemed childhood.
There was fear.
Oh and there was violence.
But sometimes blasting rays
of love would stream
through our home
giving us much needed respite
from gloom.
Mom's fear of hospitalization
so acute
that it enveloped
every move
she made.
So succinct

it had weary older aunts
write her out of the will.
Write her off
when dad breathed
his last cancerous breath.
Now nothing more than
cremated remains in the ground
and the memory of how long
it's been.

26 years is a long time.
In some countries
they release you from jail
knowing that the torment
will never heal.
That clinking key and
gruel – like food doesn't
fatten this suicide prisoner.

We look at the branches
for their strength.
Missed phone calls
for eternal silence
and double dosed pharmacist's hands
filled with perpetual
snooze buttons.
This is the wanderer
at the beach
going for the last brittle
swim.

The unnerved driver
crossing the regulated
double line.

It is the beast of compassion
that compels us to breathe
eat
love
live
and sleep.
It is the bastion
of direct denial
that smolders
like a vented viper.

Candle burns
flame flickering
its retreating light;
darkness
confirms
everything.

FRIDAY NIGHT LITE

It's been a long week.
A family reunion that
was troubling.
A bit of stumbles, slurring
and speeches.
Can't forget the speeches.
Food was fantastic
and the pain of being served
and watching the cloaked whispering.

The cat's midnight release on the floor
and the house so tight
filled with secrets
and those wanting
to just sway with some
unheard song.
It will be alright, alright.
The mosquitoes will stop their
incessant biting.
The rain will stop washing
out the driveway;
two large gashes as deep
as the Rio Grande.

We lost our first customer
to a choke.
You know the nurses tried
and the young man did

the Staying Alive shuffle
to keep him coming back.
10 minutes
and now he's gone.

A day later and it's all gone
the night as empty
as a Chevrolet purchase.
No dependable warranty
and we won't talk about
the rust.
Now after that shift
we sit down and watch
The Lost Weekend
DT's, challenges acquiring booze
and the light of day vanishing.
Small black and white screen
serving up the trembling score.
Looking for the fix.

A call two nights ago
from a quiet prison wing.
Recorded
listened to and sadly judged.
No money being sent to prevent
talking animals
and the efficacy of killing.
Just a collect call
from afar
and a computer vowing

to record

to record

to record

your incessant fright.

THERE COMES A TIME

When you must choose
between the drove of beehive work
paying bills proficiently
eating bananas on quick sale
refraining from expensive trips,
new couches
or a set of glasses.
Sometimes you have to bask
in the sweat of summer
without enough money to turn
on the fan.
Sometimes when
the classical music is playing,
my fingers slip and I break
another glass.
Sometimes people invade countries
to gain access to bragging rights
and pistols in a drawer.
Sometimes you need to give
a quarter to the recently
released mental patient.
Sometimes we have to care.

Because when you've been
brought up by Garcia Vega cigar commercials
during Bugs Bunny,
jetliners flying to freedom

not into towers,

cruises in the Caribbean

not oil spills in Alaska

line-ups at the pump

and nobody complaining,

sometimes you've got to make

that call to your Aunt

in the home.

Sometimes you've got to visit

and hug the stubbly chin

and clip her toes.

Sometimes

because pedicurists

can be so damn expensive.

Sometimes you've just got to

believe that right around the corner

you might be driving a new Olds.

That's what they told us.

There comes a time.

THEY ARE GROWING UP

It was just yesterday
that I held you in my arms.
You would both look up
with blue eyes and stare.
So much trust;
I needed that.
Having lived without trust for so long,
you both came in and believed in me.
There was no way
that I would leave you.
Checking out it is for cowards
or for calling out.
I remember the first push on the swing.
Back and forth it would go.
Gaining confidence and more trust.
Cleaning you in the bathtub;
again the trust.
Believing in yourself;
being truthful to myself.
It hurts, this frightened pain
but it has subsided.

They are growing up;
calling my name,
gathering memories in a box.
You've made the realm of living true.
You've made the possibility of love real.

You're the expression of solidarity that
your mother and I have.
We work together.
Even if squabbles occur or the baseness
of the past rears itself.

When a lightning storm strikes the North Shore,
they come wandering in the semi-darkness.
Those muffled feet;
moving cautiously between bursts of light.
They move through the living room
and up those stairs
to safety.
They are growing up
and it was just yesterday that I opened
up your memory box and remembered
the gray hairs from my chin
that you wanted to use for crafts.
Now we snuggle close.
Read from a good book
and know the value of a family
that is together.

EATING ICE CREAM ON THE PATIO

Little lips
move into lick
chocolate sprinkles
and gobbling spills.
With a pair of high pitched squeals
scoops fall
erringly to the floor.
Thank you
that it was on
the patio.

SHE GAVE ME A HUG

It is a teenage hug
from your daughter
slightly clinging
but it happens so seldom
that you welcome it
as you would one of those
recurring comets.

Thanks for bringing us dad.
I did.
Well
we did.
If you don't
you'll rock
backward and forward
and think and semi-hiss
through your teeth
I should have done that.

I did
and held her body close
to let her know
that her dad
will always be there.

O LITTLE ONE

She said that the darkness
called you.
Only 11 and already the marionette
strings begin to tighten.
It is a fear I've had since
they've been born;
both of them.

That the darkness would rise
the same pool that my mom
couldn't tread water in.
That is the fear.
It is clear
that it is at a head.
This spinning, spinning, spinning
of an 11 year old wanting to be dead.
You flipped out on the phone.
I could hear the distant shouts.
The connection was clear
but intent not entirely there.
You blamed your sister for my loss.
You blamed yourself for the weighted clothes
of a drowning boy.

Last night, I dreamt you
were in a pool
with all of your clothes on
and you were

sinking, sinking, sinking
passed your father's hand.
My shouts were muffled
in the water.
I plunged my arms in and
carried you to safety.

Those battered long eye lashes
all gone astray
because it eats at you
this venom;
they call living.

HAND COMPUTER

My son can text lines to his sister
and they giggle back and forth
emoji land and symbols.

I on the other hand
want to once again wrap my arms
around that little girl who left home.
She's a young woman in the city.
Marks at school all ablaze
and the future gleams
with shiny new floors.

In a couple of weeks
trying for her G1
that first licence in the line
of many to come.
I'm so proud of both of them
as I sit here in the forest
by a frozen lake
looking at the baffling moon
slowly rise.

A SMALL PEAR

I reach for the fruit.

It is within reach.

It is beyond reach.

It is behind a reach.

I know it is there
for I can smell it.

I can smell the pear
that has come from Argentina.

That has grown on a limb
below the equator.

That has seen different stars
and spoken to new moons.

I touch the fruit.

I smell the fruit
and taste it and let its juice
roll into my beard.

A small pear,
but a reminder
of my lover's hips.

A TORN HAMSTRING

Each morning a soft prayer.
Each day superstition grows.
Each hour his pain
of holding hands with Alzheimer's.
You can see the hurt look
of his wife.
Lines drawing deeper
carving her face into
a sphere of anxiety and sadness.
He was a hero in the war
bombing cities and civilians.
Dropping them from the chapped sky
as would a child with pennies
in a gum machine.

Years later,
they returned to the English Channel.
His plane went down
on his first mission.
He floated to safety and flew
numerous routes again.
Holding his wife's hands
they looked across the scaled water.
Military planes and boats
are performing maneuvers.
Resounding shots fired intermittently
bordering on random.

At the funeral home
people waddle in.
Hair curled,
clothes neatly pressed.
Ushers play coyly with
funerary flowers.
Flicking them into place
as would an elderly shepherd
with a stray sheep.
Singing begins,
tears of controlled madness.
Hymns played peacefully
behind a Venetian style parlor.
Murmuring of prayers
eyes gently reddening,
memories.

If life's only sting of pain
could be felt
pulling a hamstring,
playing ball
with your son.

CLIMBING A CALIFORNIAN HILL

I went with three young ladies
and my son for a hike.
It was in the desert so you
had to watch for rattlers.
We went on ahead.
My son wearing a yellow shirt
and I following in a yellow
Swedish hat.
I have letter carried in -40C.
I have biked 30 KM routes
but nearing the top of this pass
my breath was rapid.
My son asked;
Are you OK?

In billygoat fashion
he climbed
but waited for me.
The view over the valley
was spectacular,
incredible.
We took deserved sips of water
and switch-backed
down the hill
before the sun
became oppressive
and rattlers start
to shake.

SKATE PARK, PALM SPRINGS

Went for a walk;
a long one with my son.
He pedals on his scooter
and I holding his growing hand.
Sometimes he goes ahead.
This time really hot,
feet using shoes that
have been barely broken in.

I see the transients
gathering in clusters at the park
near the library.
They gravitate to the shade.
Shopping carts full
but no check-out line
because these
are hauled with them
forever.
I see bottles of water,
empties
a chess board
a game of Monopoly
and that long ago stare
that comes from living
day to day.

Heat is oppressive.
I come from the cold

this is another kind of demon.
Pushing those clanging shopping carts
their lives in front of them
wheeled in a steel bucket.
What do you suppose that 3 iron is for?
We get to the skate park
and they won't allow scooters
only on Wednesdays.
So we grumbly walk back home
vowing to return
to let those sweet wheels
just spin.

DANIEL'S GONE

He was going over
for a trial
with a Swedish club for soccer.
He called and said;
They want me dad.
I'm staying.

Now the second leg
of the flight is left empty.
He tucks himself in at night
and I the father who loves
that little boy
goes in and out of his room
like a dog waiting
for you
to come home.

CIRCLING THE NEST

I go into your room
it is empty.
As empty as your sister's room
almost two years ago.

Now we can watch
whatever we want.
Read books to each other.
Tickle each other silly.
Swim in the lake
and skate on the ice at night.

Now I know what
it's like when they leave.
The way it tears at my skin
those photographs,
that you can almost inhale.

We brought them up to fly.
The two of them bravely boarding
those yellow school buses.
We hid the tears until
they were out of sight.
Now I know what it's like
when you don't hear
the laughter.

COMING UNDONE

His small cleats
would always loosen.
He'd go down on one knee
and tie them up again.

Now he's across the Atlantic
following his dream.
Putting balls at the feet
of teammates.

When a log goes into the flame,
bark comes undone
and flares up
fast.

So too
did this father
leaving a 16 year old son
to board a plane
alone.

Who's coming undone?

TRAIN WHISTLE

On the hill a propeller spins.
It gathers energy from the past
and rotates,
giving a new perspective
after each lap.

In this village I lived as a boy.
Crossing the county boundaries and
being chased at school
for being different.
I know all about being out of breath
and on the run.
It's come full circle;
this trip.
It is an understanding
that has come from being
in your grandmother's small room
and looking out.
Sometimes a murder of crows
covers the sky.
It supplies the eyes with a variance
and let all numbness rise.

Other times a train whistle
startles the stillness
and brings home
the rusty nails
being driven in

with a shackled pick
and a weightless father.

Counting the whistles
I can hear the voices come trailing
across the sky.
Covering my ears
my mouth opens and releases
a colossal scream.
My lips quiver gently
as I let the wind return
and blow the bombastic past
out over the hills
and to the sea.

I THOUGHT I WAS CLAIRVOYANT

But all it was,
was another word for uneasy.
It comes,
this feeling.
A feeling of some conquest that needs to be
fulfilled,
yet all that is craved,
but a moment of silence in this nocturnal
and neon world.

I know that it is easy to offshoot the poet
for they don't see things as most people do.
It is like they've smoked too many drugs
or inhaled enough glue
or attempted death too many times;
that their eyes glow in the dark
like scared llamas.
I know for one that I try my best to be normal.
Now I can't tell you every day how well the Dow
did
or how many points the NASDAQ went up or
down
but I can tell you about sports.

As a kid I would hide in the box scores.
I would memorize them frontward and
backward.
It would help me forget about the desperate time

in our house.
It would help me forget about my mother's
plaguing madness
and my father's inane way of dealing with it.
So I would curl up and read those box scores.
They were like old friends
acquaintances that you wanted to keep up.
I would caress the numbers
as they would stop some of the suffering
if but briefly.
I would eat up the tiny stories
of mini-accomplishments of
sacrifice and denial.
I really understood these stars
far better than I did the stars up in the sky.
They were real to me.
They were my closet-full of facts
that could keep me amused for hours.
Some kids liked marbles
or comic books
but I liked those box scores.
They helped
and to this day in time of need,
I return to them.
It gets the axle back in place.
It puts the seat in a more comfortable position
but it needs those eyes to glance over it.
To feel that something is going to chance;
that there is always a tomorrow.

No matter how many rain delays
or closed airports.

I thought I was clairvoyant,
but I realize now that
it is another word for abdicator.
Keeper of lost souls
and tempered dreams.
They live in the box score
and will always
be the same
when it ends
5 – 3.

RUSTED ROSE

Clinking the #13,
I indulge in a quest
for a clear night of dreams.
Shuddering left
a year ago.
It flitted away
like a post-humus eulogy.
It sounds forced,
fake and disconnected.
Grappling my love of survival,
I coax the sheer shame
locked inside my coals
and ask for an optical clear lens.
Music beckons beneath
my rigid tongue.
I want to laugh
in my lover's presence.
Not to see some dusted over
Memorial ceremony.
Streams of two-timing faces
shaking my betrayed hand.
They cling to that last gasp
she uttered to her admirers.
I calmly read from the Bible.
The words come clearly
but leave me

with an uncommon
emptiness.

I cling to the hope
that music could stage
a ceremonial departure.
Instead,
I remain calm,
in my terror-ridden world,
watching wringed socks dry
on an overworked heater.
I shall cut my hair
letting each empty strand
float to the naked floor.
I will free
the scent of coffins
from my nostrils.
It will be replaced
with a loving, cherished
and forgiving rose.

KEEP TALKING

That's what the Premier
of my province was told by
his grandmother
on his wedding day.
Even when that road gets so rough.
Even when struggling decisions
are burrowed into your choices.
You need to keep talking.

It took great courage to tell
how you felt.
That is wasn't all it was supposed to be.
Head of your school
on the verge of being captain of your team,
changing schools so you could learn
another language.
You followed your spike of learning.
You stood in front of all
at the Legion and spoke
of Band-aids.
It does heal the spirit.
Keep talking.
You're afraid of me.
The same fear I had of my own father.

They said it was for the best.
That fear brought control.
It was just the opposite.

The latch of safety was opened
when my parents left.
I was 14 and 19.
I still shake my head.
I shake and shake and shake it
trying to control the seizure
that comes every so often
when I'm unprepared.

It's time to be a kid.
Pressure needs an outlet.
Keep talking.
My brave son,
we'll find each other
in that continuous mist.
Keep talking
and I'll hold you
as we both did
when you were a little infant
in that incubator.
I'll keep talking, reading
and being with you.

PITCH BLACK MORNING

I stumble freely
wanting to not step
on the cat.
It is Sunday morning
almost 6:00 am.
Hey I slept in.
I found Vold,
a Norwegian poet
and read him gently.
Sorrow is around the room
but it remains inside of us.
Deep inside.

Passed the woman laying flowers
on her husband's grave.
Passed the grandmother looking
out a 3rd floor window
the silence pressing in.
Passed the child
finding a dead butterfly
the wings no longer opening
colors drifting away.
Passed the hunter in a blind
in early morning waiting
to pull that tired trigger
again wanting
that long stick

to heat up
in his hands.
Passed the accident
policeman taking numbers and names
trying to recreate the past
and beyond that turmoil
silence reigns.

It is in this sphere
that healing commences.
Truant sorrow falls
rapidly and the walls open
the sun tries to speak
through solemn
shifting clouds.

SLY CIGARETTE

Raising that little black box,
plastic wrap crinkled,
reminding every ex-smoker
of that found one in the night.
Tax-free smells.
Tobacco, perfume, liquor
are reminders of the beauty
we hold entranced.
Slick, studied ads
slide down our main streets.
Nicotine craving onscreen.
Deny alcohol and you deny existence.
Cover up that bodily scent
with chemicals and
rows of dead rabbits, parrots
who know the meaning
of wearing perfume every day.
Sulking in our 4 walled rooms,
TV blaring the weather,
coated lies cover up the truth
of dirty fingers, expiring livers
and frequent body rashes.
We live in a crowded dream
that lies somewhere between
channel 24 and 72.

COFFEE IN THE MORNING

At 4:47 am
that alarm;
work clothes laid out the night before
as it's always a little foggy.
Read a couple of pages
of a comic football serial
that I used to devour as a child.

Now at 46
I read stories of strife
heroism
conquest
and the drama of
realizing
youthful dreams.
Now they are the collective lottery tickets
bought at work.
Daily swims when weather permitting
and a dark cup of coffee
I make for my lover and friend.

This is living the dream
of realizing that it doesn't have
to be hard
at least not all the time.

PHONY

When someone says I've got
a fibbing problem
then bless them for they have given me
an insight into the soul
that I've missed.
I could handle the coffins
and maggots eating the dead fish.
The smell of rotting dog
could perk up my day.
Rolling under the graffiti filled bridge
a girdled joint of insanity;
fouls the hopeless turmoil.
Hog wash
Pork rinds
Grits
All the delicious savory curbs
of dismissal that crawl in my curdling skin.
Phony, phony, phony

Because I play the stocks on the side
I'm phony.
Because I have a chance to do what I really
want to do then I'm a phony.
To say that it never would have happened
had I not had a surgical advance of funds.
Well,
if you must know

it took some ole fashioned timely deaths
to convince my Postmaster that I was writing
more than just roses are red poems.

Having enemas as punishment
or that twisted coat hanger
all hold that phony past
into an omnipresent truth.
I was choked when I skipped school.
I was taunted with a GREASE 8 track
dangling on a string from the ceiling
as an encouraging reminder of why
I should get A's.
And people wonder why I got out of the
collapsing locks.
When I realize that the view from within
is just as pretty as the insomniacs window
I fall on my knees and give thanks to sanity.
Keeping the fires of hatred
is finally subsiding
as is the swallowing pain
of giving grace.

TWO WAKES IN A WEEK

It's the line-ups
and clammy hands
guest book that needs to be signed
photos placed on boards
lovingly displayed with laughter,
hugs and memories captured
with a click.
On the wall is a TV screen
with a loop,
those same photos
scrolling
subtly coming alive.
So that's what the world looked like
in black and white.
There are speeches at one
and always the ever present Christian tales
helping loved ones cope
with the sudden
and unknown.
People mumble
The Lord's Prayer
under their breath
some don't know the words
as its been taken
out of the schools.

You see images of yourself

in these gatherings
what will it look like when I go
will the room be full
or half empty
who'll do the catering
or will the Church Ladies kind hands
make those tuna, egg salad
and SPAM sandwiches?

You hug those you know
and a far away handshake
for those you don't.
The flowers try to mask the scent of death
but it's there.
It's always there.
Even with the cremated.
There must be some
scratch and sniff sticker
that captures it.
Reverence
sustained fear
and the two fold sadness
of leaving the safety of the brood.

You shuffle your feet
as some opt to give
in memory of gifts
to carry on legacies,
start new projects
or just remain sustainable.

As humans we've always sheltered
the fright of being alone.
Some find out too late before others
see the clarity at the end.
When the pressures of work
are eradicated.
The dead are rendered meaningless
unrealized dreams
just that
unrealized dreams.

It makes you think
two wakes in a week
that to follow that curly spire
to the sky
round and round
keeping those sinister
and fragile flames
at bay.

STATUE IN THE FOREST

That's where I will be buried.
Behind her blessed bottom
overlooking the lake.
It isn't far
from the house.
Not many flowers needed.
The pine needles will keep
me warm.

My son mockingly says;
I won't bury you there,
and I joke that;
If you don't
I'll come back
and haunt you.

Now we brush away the leaves
watch the sun
through the trees
and are thankful
for every breath
every day.

SALIVATING GHOSTS

She chuckles her sly cough
and watches me poke
at those keyboards of my past.
I roll every vowel and letter from these
encumbered alphabets,
but the solution to those experiences seems
to shy away in some pre-marital fear.
The veils of this world have
all been lifted showing
the most vile mascara
running clouds of tepid streams
as unwanted tears.
They fold the faces in total absence of
the naked presence
one feels when fully nude.

Maybe if it hadn't have been for her
quasi-holistic questions,
my responsive 12 year old cock
might have remained asleep,
untouched,
like some hibernating bear.

Instead her breath
would slither into my ear,
holding me at the edge of my own
sense of sanity.
Coddling me near

that abyss of pre-ejaculatory release,
she'd coax me to stay in between
her plush bosom
of hatred.

Many men turned down her advances.
The only gift that remained
when her breast slagged
was the small joy of her holding one's own
in the ring.
She had a master trainer,
whose name I'll never know
but I am convinced exists.
The nape of my inner sanctum
would be fondled as if all
who found that lost fountain of youth
could drink from the sacred water.
No, my friends.
The price you pay for such unruly realism
is betwixt two bosoms and monster thighs.
The caverns of hope remain
in cysts of red blood.
There is no light at the end of those tunnels.
Only lost children,
screaming trapped emotions
when scrapes and coat hangers peel the fat.
I always knew when to duck.
Betrayal is sweetest when
stroked alone.

It takes an All-American school boy to
please a nymphomaniac mother.
Pin a purple stripe
on that lapel,
sergeant.

WHAT IS THIS FACE?

The one looking back from
the mirror
slightly grayer
with long strands all tizzy
and unglued.
No toupee here.
No soup kitchen Thanksgiving smile.
This isn't some 16 year old
loin shriek.
This isn't a reckless abandoned will
where countesses counted
gardeners.
This wail of ageing
has always existed.

But a neutered dog
too tired to bark;
breath a putrid
uncleaned compost bucket.
Panting at the cotton underwear
too tired to sniff.
They say scent
is the last
to go.

The pain was a 12 on a scale
of 1 to 10.
It had burst two weeks prior.
In grand Viking fashion,
I soldiered on and nearly
collapsed at work.

I knew I must get to a doctor
and I chose the one hour drive
to my physician
in the town of Perth.
I used to letter carry there
and that's a good thing
as he'd moved offices.
After a hurried examination
he said to go to emergency.
I'll let them know you're coming
and don't stop at Tim Horton's.

Do you know how challenging
a recovering alcoholic
has to explain
that morphine
is not an option?
I relented to a couple of millilitres.
Before the ambulance ride
3 little lights going off.
The one in the middle meant brake

and more pain.

I met the surgeon
5:00 pm surgery
to remove my appendix.
After jumping on the train from Toronto,
my beautiful wife came.
I held her hand.
Mine was immensely clammy.
They wheeled me to await the surgery.
I saw the surgeon prepping
and I heard a 70's sitcom laugh track.
I'm glad he's calm.
Those studio audience laughs doing their job.

I signed a last form and then
into the theatre.
The lights and antiseptic smell
and the arm out to my left.
Not like the ones at the end
in Texas
on death row.
Those are both arms wide
almost Christ like.
Anesthetist pushed the capsule
over my bearded chin
I breathed in
and then that bed
began spinning.

NO MORE LIZARDS

Waking up in the middle of the night
catheter firmly placed
they sent some drugs down into my veins.
It's for the pain,
she whispered
in the semi-dark room.
Have a nice trip.

The lizards were almost upon me.
Crawling out of the ceiling,
Crawling across my bed,
up the panting walls
and then breasts covered all
and then the erection with a catheter.
There are clubs for that sort of thing
in Berlin.
Not for me.
They wanted to re-administer
the next morning
but no
I'd rather have the pain.

No more lizards
please.

When you've got tubes hanging out of you
you try your damndest to put
a Viking step in front of another.
Nurses notice
that I'm breaking out
yet again.

My son comes to visit.
His face is firm but he doesn't
relinquish eye contact.
I'll help you;
he says.
We walk down the aisles
not to be married off
not to be sent into some final
resting place
not to be seen as weakness.
It's OK dad;
and his growing hand
envelops my clammy one
and in relative silence
we place one foot
in front of the other.

IN BED; WINTER

The cat is meowing.
There are two pitches.
One for food
the other for
I need to crap.
Meowing persists.
No, I really need to crap.

I jump out of bed
in my Björn Borg underwear
and let her out.
Doing the winter dance
so she can scratch
to be let back in.

A CAT'S MEOW

I need to shit.
That's the tone that comes
 from the 12 year old bitty.
It's -40C outside the same as -40F
only one word to say
cold.
She can't shit
only going outside
and then the meows of let me in
persistent and then clawing at the door.
Not a week and a half ago
barely able to walk
I lay down on the bed
and when I awoke from my drugged daze
she was curled up at my feet
to keep them warm.
My boss told me;
They know…

So if you have to clean up
a little turd now and then
that's the price of animals
that's the price of caring.

WALKING IN THE SNOW

I put on my orange boots.
No socks on.
I haven't been outside for
almost 8 days.
When I inhaled the air
it was as fresh
as that first white sheet
on the line
in Spring.
Birds were flitting around
the feeder.
I got up to the road.
I was searching for wood
for next winter.
The plight of a Canadian
on the land.
This Spring I want to give back.
We'll get trees from the local nursery
and replant.
It's time to rejuvenate the forest
that is blanketed
ever so quietly
with snow.

When it's cold in Canada
your testicles go burrowing for warmth
our nostrils freeze
especially those nostril hairs
you put your hands together that the car
will start
you hope the water will still run.
Always leave a little drip
to keep the line open.
You get the wood in,
wood I can't lift and roll each one
individually across the floor.
Place them, fizzing
all day
mixing up the heat because that's
what you swim towards in your mind.
Your toes so cold from too many cigarettes
in your teens.
Your fingers crack from delivering the mail.
Even attempting erotic massage,
the hands close and little crackles
fill the sheets.

You get into the car and visit
the surgeon.
Your only outing for almost a week
and the ride is bumping the scars
you just grit your teeth and

grab the holy shit handles.

We got it all son
including a carcinoid growth that
was benign.

Soon as I hear a word that sounds like cancer
I wonder.
I remember that Christmas,
the striped blue and white bathrobe
and dad in quiet tears
untangling the lights for the tree
for the last time.

When it's cold up here
in this Canadian North
that's when those tired of fighting
leave
check out
not paying any more bills
just that funeral when they can dig
down in the Spring again.

Nick Cave comforts
as a cat quietly snores
logs crackle
and an unwanted scented candle
burns
keeping the encompassing dark
briefly
ever so briefly
at bay.

HARD ON IN A CHAIR

It's bold to see a picture
of yourself
with an erection
seated in a brown antique chair
glasses still on
as if you need glasses to see.
It's a photo that says
virility
long before any snips.
It still stands at attention.
Well most of the time.
I find the key is to just relax
and that's not an easy thing to do
but relax
because that frothy release
and subsequent drastic drool
just anesthetic
this middle aged man
chasing the cloud
of some constant
R.E.M sleep.

I couldn't make the moves.
I'd tried the day before.
I remember
as an 11 year old
that when I went to Germany
representing Canada
our leader's job was helping handicapped
people have sex.
Why shouldn't they?

Well I tried yesterday.
Well during sex it's usually we.
She was so caring.
My hands a little fumbly.
My over protectiveness
of the mottled scars.
Instead we tried from behind
I on my toes
trying my best to be that young bull
and she kindly encouraging.
I'm no Hemingway
wanting to blow it all away
when it doesn't work.
It will be hard
but with the right amount of moistness
and the right angle
it can happen.

LEAVING THE FLUFFED NEST

Last night
my wife drove me
to the local high school
to watch Peter Pan.
Recovering from surgery
this was my first real outing
of any kind of excitement
since the ambulance ride.
The stage was set in the gym
and it was ornate
with many scene changes,
a few musical numbers
and the story of a young boy
who never wants
to grow up.

Sitting there
my wife leaned into me
and her shoulder softly touched mine.
It felt as if I was back at the movies
when I took her out on a date
and we didn't see one movie
but two.

The scenery of children dancing around
fighting pirates
and time.
I sat there

and after awhile
uncomfortably
as the stitches were tugging
and the chair was hard
but that was fine
because she leaned into me
again
and inside
I sighed.
There comes a time
when it's OK
to finally grow up.

OFFICE FULL OF BOXES

Opening the first batch
there are tax files
going back
10 years.
You can pitch them
after 6.
I prefer the funeral pyre way
letting fly up the chimney
and straying into ash.
The next box was pictures.
Nude ones
of my lover.
We do things when we are young.
Before the scars
before the lines
maybe that's why they want
the nice cameras from Playboy
to capture those poses
those sepulchral sultry eyes
and arid curves.
But this,
this is my lover
and she still gives
that same excitement
with a little kiss
before noon.

IT'S HARD TO SLEEP

It is the week after Christmas.
Those who want to shop
have gone to the malls
others sit in pyjamas
and purchase
that anxiety release
with a click
of their finger.

Here I am
up at 5:00 am
again
body still used to moving
parcel after parcel
letter after letter
to satisfy the hunger
and need
to somehow belong.

They send their medical forms
passport renewals
returned items of
tight fitting clothing
and I just smile
a sometimes
unwarranted smile

and wrap my arms
around the garbage can
and trudge up the driveway
for the weekly dispersal.

ADJUSTING THE ALARM

It is always at night,
a couple of pushes
and double checks to see
if it's on.
If it will work.
Now in adulthood
the concept of time
so rigid.
Doors opening
customers being served
and then that 4:47 am
beeping
that spirals into your dream.

One of old acquaintances
taking your grandmother's
blood pressure
she forgot to take those pills
again.

Now the house is almost silent.
Our daughter has left
for the city.
Neon attracts so much.
Not just bugs spiralling into death
as our neighbor in the burbs
had a bug zapper.
It would make noises all night

each crackle another death
along the highway we call life.

It's like that with friends.
Soon their parents are poorly
and then that causal dream
that is jumbled and played with
a puppy licking
your sleeping face.
That alarm sounds it's,
I'm here
a fused warning
and regretfully
and respectfully
you follow the well-worn path
to the shower
and that days'
impending doom.

Sans l'alarme.
C'est fini.

TALKING ABOUT THE SHADOW

It is in board rooms across
the land.
Opaque, gleaming beauty
of making the grade.
Delivering on time.
No snow days here.
You must scrub
to get these dishes clean.
You swirl with the jaundiced vision
of more and more and more
and then in its cylindrical madness
there is nothing.
The penultimate lie.
The non-winning ticket crumpled in the yard.
The little tassel on your cap
to say that you've done really well.
Now submit
and just try to pay it back.
The lost moments when studying
the lost lines when vomiting
what the question is really asking of you.

This quelled search is but a dream.
A sweaty one mind you.
But nonetheless as crammed and culled
at the frail belief that comes
from losing god-like vision before two.

Now the stumbling is ensconced
with the vitality of zebra stripes
and that fainting prayer
of not this time,
not this time
for I have you.

THERE ARE SOME THINGS THAT NEED EXPLAINING

Why all new titles of books have
a reference to girls
Why after two years of hard academic study
under an IB program must she wait
Why people next to you on a flight
have nothing to say
Why the cat runs out when you're about
to leave for the day
Why some clowns feel compelled
to pass snowplows
Why a President is elected by the people
and he's mean
Why certain men with a little bit of power
are prone to cruelness
Why some soccer players
can take a penalty
and others can't
Why it takes so long to open up
bank accounts in Denmark
Why feelings of remorse surface
when porn is used to release
Why smiles often hide the trace meaning
of compatibility and the essence
of companionship one sees in a dog
Why don't the politicians quit fibbing
and do the right thing

Why it takes visiting dead people abroad
levels the emotional playing field
Why is it that on a flight between
Chicago and San Francisco
that the palpitations arise
and leave you stunned
Why does writing calm that section
of the cerebrum
Why are so many suicides in books
and the silence about incest
Why are the sandwiches so expensive
at the airport
Why the need for popcorn in Chicago
Why do people drive their cars
distractedly on the freeway

There needs to be
some explaining
while trucks of illegals
are turned back
children cry repeatedly
at having their mother taken away.
It's not too much of a stretch
to see those cattle cars
filled again.

MEETING A FELLOW DEADHEAD

So here we are
years later
those rollicking tunes
spinning girls
long haired boys,
patchouli around every bend
hands moving like butterflies
finally the right petal
wings vacant, fluttering
and then
stop.

It is at Wit's End
that the futon is my home.
I lay down my head
no more strike threats
no more new hires to welcome
no more audits to prepare
no more routes needing annual inspections
no more whines of I'm not feeling well

Sometimes we all feel that sickly
sooty slide
We need a place to dream
We need to feel a well-timed sizeable hug
We need the body to rest
and in this blessed basement
surrounded by Grateful Dead colors
I sleep the sleep
of the free.

OH FIREMAN MY FIREMAN

I'm having trouble breathing
Call 911
Who is the first to respond?
You.
You drop the hammer, chain, log, pen
paintbrush and get into your fueled vehicle
parked for the ready
colored lights flashing
and you find Mrs. Astor struggling.
All those nights of training
being away from family
again,
so others can live.
That is sacrifice.
That is the calming blanket
around the shocked devastated home owner.
You've seen it.
Hardened steel cutting away to extract bodies
like some toughened tooth that needs
a specialist from away.
Those specialists are you.

At parades, that red fire engine buffed so clean
almost a reminder of can it ever get truly clean
with that smoke pumping out of the houses veins.
You rub and rub and rub and then remember the laughs
of obstacle courses at school year end parties.

You pull children to safety from cold water.

You help grandma get that kitty down from the old
oak tree.

You check batteries in fire alarms.

Oh Fireman my Fireman.

You are the epitome of team.

All working to put out a blaze;

slow a running heart

lift a troubled soul.

When others run from the house

you run into that cloud.

Hoses on the ready

double checked tanks on your back.

The older ones let the young pups

get that blackened glare

of seeing the unspeakable.

Car wrecks warranting a road closure.

Those taking their lives and then

that lost stare

of returning home to cold suppers

vaguely reheated

in a troubled microwave oven.

You've even seen those explode too.

You are all one.

The cross on your helmet;

some embedding that cross

into their flesh.

You are the saving wings

as we see

those caring eyes

those sometimes wild eyes

those saddened eyes

of sacrifice.

Oh Fireman my Fireman.

We thank you.

A SHOT IN GOTHENBURG

He's returned again.

Plastic man from the States.

800 entourage strong.

Oil firing his thin veins.

They talk of Kyoto.

They talk of missile defense systems.

They talk of the transient New World Order.

Nothing solved.

Media delivers cute lines.

Nothing was decided.

Translation;

the kind of talk that happens before a divorce.

Outside the demonstrators gather

with slogans and effective chants.

Seemingly never seen or heard on television,

only references to *protesters*

and size and strength of police.

One live bullet.

Fired into the crowd.

A 19-year-old falls.

One of the professionals.

Dogs, police, batons,

cobbled rocks hurled at bank machines

and McDonald's.

This is madness.

This is the sting of a plated union

between multi-national and puppet government

fed to us by journalists on the nod.
In Gothenburg there were 200 journalists.
5 were American.
Bush answered 4 questions from the 5.
You talk of a circus.
This is a well-filed staff
that hammers any resistors.
It crushes any opposition.
It justifies brutality by police.
The inherent madness begins
when the boiling youth
tired of parents being laid-off yet again
tired of companies not paying fair wages
tired of student loans out of control
tired of the environment being neglected and ignored
tired of being left out of meetings
tired of secrecy
tired of being bullied by elders
tired of banks loaning money to the rich
tired of obedience
tired of the Trans-national transport of schooling
tired of freedom paid by larger forces of security
tired of genetically altered food
tired of animals being burned because of inept
farming practices
tired of censorship
tired of claustrophobic testing of children in order to
place them in society
tired of concessions and political needs

tired of useless and dated diplomacy
tired of conspiracy
tired of votes decided with a 51% majority
tired of recounts
tired of lies
tired of poisoned water and tainted seas
tired of nuclear testing
tired of cloning
tired of trademarks
tired of the stadium of fear that lead untrained officers
to shoot live bullets in the dark.

This time they succeeded in dispersing the crowd.
But rest assured,
like in France
fighting for the right to bread;
they'll return crazed
in greater numbers.

CAPTAIN LANCE

As the locks slowly go up
you wait patiently
as you always have
for that freedom that
a boat on water gives.
Here you are Captain Lance
you share journeys
with guests and friends
travelling with your assured guidance.

You always knew Lance,
when a deal was good
and you just had to tell someone.
You knew the beauty of sunsets
in Portland
not only in summer
but in winter too.
You knew that opening your home
was done with style.
You knew the power of cleaner engines
even though some still can't
believe that it's true.

But it is Lance
and now as families gather
by the shore
and take pictures of growing children;
you my friend have revealed to me

that the best captains
are hard to find.

You taught me to believe
in my gut and follow a vision
however blind it may seem.
Captain Lance
your boat will always
be seen across the bay
carrying the shadows of evening
carrying the joy that you brought
to family and friends
carrying us all
safely
home.

SMELLING THE BACON FAT

It is a distinct brunch smell.

It is a memory that soothes and fades.

It is a controlled laugh or a misguided question.

It is a father on life support and lungs collapsing.

It is the thin razor blades of a troubled teenager.

It is a bottle of valium and a bottle of gin.

It is a lukewarm shower
to shed yesterday's skin.

It is the power of a child's cry
to evoke tears of laughter.

It is a black and white TV rotting in a landfill.

It is a junkyard of differing parts
dolled out among rows of automobiles.

It is a motel room with pubic hair on the floor.

It is a turbulence filled flight.

It is a dog biting at a lecherous sore.

It is a pubis filled with love.

It is a disgruntled postal worker delivering admail.

It is a bucket of sorrow in baskets of rain.

It is a day of rejoicing
when the smell cakes your senses.

You know that last night's fuck was real
and that it was all
nothing
but good.

BRITISH SMILE

I chipped my tooth in Denmark.
On the run at the post office
while on the bike delivering
packages and mail.
I found solace
in a sheltered stairwell.

At times
I would hear voices from the apartments
other times footsteps
or laughter in the yard.
I was so hungry
that I bit into my spoon
and chipped two teeth.

Now back on Canadian soil
2 trips to the dentist
to fix them.
I'm not sure if this time
I dislodged the fixin'
with a tube down my throat
and the anesthesiologist
or if it was that wad
of toffee from Christmas;
a British treat
chewing madly to loosen its hardness
and now as I look into the mirror
I can truly say with utter conviction

that the last bite

has just given me

a dislodged,

wry

and jaunty

British smile.

WOODEN DANGER SIGN

There is a little dip
as one backs into the parking lot
at the post office
in Manotick.
There used to be a tree that
would guide the mail truck in
as they would
beep, beep, beep
in place.
It was cut down
nothing but a stump
kind of what's left
of your will
working with mounds of mail
grunts of fellow workers
and teetering parcels.

That danger sign is well placed.
People walking
stop
and can't seem to see
the danger.
They don't see the truck
sideways in the ditch
in the dark
men and women unloading
at an angle

Canadian Tire Wish Catalogues
bundle after bundle.

On the other side
of the building
they've placed
a large sign
wanting drivers.
Those willing to work with
sweat
time lines
and snide remarks
of *Can't you read?*

I think the new danger sign
flows across
the whole property.
The one in blackness
at 6:50 am.
Safety lights shining out
disturbing the neighbors
the key and code
justly inserted,
pressed
waiting
to be
let in.

SELLING A STAMP

It takes a certain one
to sell stamps
because they are small pieces
of peel-able stickers that
are placed on letters of
secrecy.
A tongue is used to displace
the bill, love letter, crushed
income tax forms into the mail.
You can listen to the stories
or just try to drown out
the sadness.
Widows walking daily to that little
locked box and finding
a temporary solace of being
added to some advertiser's list.
Some throw them away in disgust
others relish the thought of
being included again
as on the school yard
when they were picking teams.
Some single mothers have left
those who cheat and will cheat
until death will cheat them.
One who is always late with
the child support payments.
Excuses pile up like paper napkins

ready for the dispenser.
Each one torn off
and gets discarded after
a little sniffle.
There are tourists visiting,
wanting to tell home
of beauty in trees, lakes and highways.
Scribbling lines and mocking pictures
sent through the system
to cheer some Aunts and Uncles
they haven't seen since
Christmas.
You are selling registered letters,
to burly men waiting to hound
ex-wives and test the boundaries
of restraining orders.
You deal with lazy Fed Ex employees
wanting directions
and by law you give them none.
You sell coins to those wanting
to capture a moment in time.
A birthday, anniversary or special gift
for yourself.
They will grow dusty in the vaults
across the land and will help someone
with a future student loan,
or a down payment on a new TV.
Risking all,
they tell their fears,

hatred and love in a hushed,
priestly tone and sometimes
when you leave the office,
after successfully putting those
printed sheets away,
you feel an urgency to shout,
or cry
or scream at shadows
that creep into the hands
of those willing
to sell stamps.

THE OVERBURDEN

It's the trees on top
then lilies, lilacs
and reeds.
It's what's removed by big machines
in order to dig deeper into the earth.
Extracting oil, gas and rub a dub coal.
The term used is overburden.
What kind of Orwellian doublespeak
is this?
What will it take to change the minds
of those 1%?
I think I know.
Now I never said it was going to be easy.

In a room
you put together
the power of a hockey mom
who sees a bad call
you need the fear of a father
watching his daughter crumple to the ice
and lay on it for more than 20 minutes
because they've cut back on ambulatory care
then you sprinkle in a raging moose
about to protect its young
you throw in some
Maalox to smear on your face
because they just love

to shoot canister after canister
of the gas.
Then in Southern India
you need at least two deaths
at the hands of rifled police
trying to contain the crowd.
You mix in a video from China
about asking a child if they've ever seen a cloud
or if they know what blue sky looks like.
You put that on a video that gets
200 million hits before
the Chinese government
shuts it down.
You add in a President who has brought
all the holes his nation is drilling
proud of the products and
crowing the end
justifies the means.
You add a pinch of Greek outrage
when a Canadian gold company
plunders land in the name of stabilizing
an economic market.
Then you release a hurricane on New York.
Once the floods hits the streets
FEMA having been plundered
then all that is left is but a small press release
from those brilliant souls at Heartland.
Now top it off with a nervous rendition
of Idle No More at your local mall

and what do you get.

It starts with the overburden.
That word is correct
because the stale way that we've
taken, taken, taken
has come to its final end.
Water and air is something
we all consume.
It crosses those lined man made borders
and hopefully without surgical masks
that have been put in place
by overworked doctors.
By linking hands,
feet,
arms
ideas
that's what really,
really
scares them.
Because in the end when you
truly have nothing
then in grand Western
head scratching
how can we do this fashion
you fight not with weapons
not with staged rage
but that 4 letter word that
encompasses us all.

Love.
That's where X
has always
marked the spot.

UNFORTUNATELY, THANKS FOR EVERYTHING

It's in the back of the drawer,
beside the batteries
exposing themselves.
Don't touch your eyes.
It's at the bus stop
waiting with your daughter,
holding her hand
yellow bus letting go.
It's the vehicle
where you lost your virginity
stain so hard
to get out.
It's in the questions asked
by curious teachers
of how she did it?
How she left
and what a tragedy?
It is in the books that are read
reams of them
trying to find clues
some threads
but mostly more distance.
It is in the sliding doors
at a hospital
questions asked
telephone interruption

I'm with a patient
Not now.
Need to focus
I didn't tell anyone
where I was going.
It's in the calmed
controlled cough of your
cancerous father.
Not trying to frighten
but you know the crowd
wants to know
that's why they tune in.
It's the trees cut outside
your home.
The ones shading the light
not exposing the secrets
now barren
as a troubled womb.
It's the first time you see tubes
surgery complete
resting required
not sure of the mood.
It is the balance of politics
of conveying trust
yet yielding none,
that brittle sphere
of closed sessions
carried successfully
to the tomb.

It is the worried dreams of youth
will the planet melt
the sun freeze
the day going boom?

Now it is that silent flower
at the gravesite in a Swedish town.
Raking the stones
to maintain some order.
Almost Japanese in its design
but thoughtfully
your voice treads across
lit tombstones.
Candles lighting the vastness
feet truncated
placing the dying bouquet
and flight.
Unfortunately,
no job
as you don't speak the language
you don't give hints
of understanding the culture.
Sometimes lives can be understood
and it is only then
that the crisis of
following turbulent dreams
drowns
in a pool by the lake.
Clothes too heavy

breathing scattered
filling ducts with fluid.
Heartbeat irregular
then none
none at all.
Unfortunately
thanks for everything,
the taste of dhal
before noon.

ACKNOWLEDGMENTS

I would like to thank John Brantingham for inviting me to Mt. SAC Writer's Festival where I had a chance to meet Mark Givens on a panel. That connection made this publication happen. I want to thank Suzanne Marsden with the cover design. Having worked with Marsden on my first chapbook back in the mid 90's her artwork and ideas have always inspired me. I still remember the day Bukowski died and she painted and I wrote at her apartment. Our daughter Emilia had a chance to go through and catch Danish spelling. I want to thank the poetry appreciation group at Tarnby Bibliotek for their support. During our two year stay in Copenhagen that once a month meeting with that group was vital for both sanity and acceptance into the local culture. I remember the first day I walked into the room they all looked up and one exclaimed ; "*It's a man...!*" They had never had a man in their group before. I also want to thank Mark Givens for publishing this book. The courage to make a big collection is thanks to Mark.

It was at Don and Cathy McCullough's house is where I made the final selection of poems. They were off camping and I took care of their two cats for a week. It was forced solitude almost like when I was at The Helene Wurlitzer Foundation so many years ago. It made the mind focus and in between persistent meows to be fed that the work percolated and the sometimes challenging topics germinated until the words funneled into the work you see today.

Also Daniel and Emilia for being there and game for new adventures. Julie for looking after our home when we were in Denmark and loving the woods as much as I do. Thank you to Susanne and Winnie for being the best Danish welcoming committee and friends a family could ever have. They were there to give guidance and force when hurdles needed jumping and persistence was tantamount. I want to close in saying a big thank you to Vicki without the support of whom I wouldn't have had the courage to write about the unmentionable. Having had challenges in my youth, my pen was the driving catalyst to make it through to another day. So many years later and we are still together having had the courage to raise children, follow dreams overseas and realize that though the past casts an immense shadow one must always push for that elusive light.